D1287901

Chronology

Dossier Series
ISBN 978-1-946433-02-2
First Edition, First Printing, 2018
Second Printing, 2020

Ugly Duckling Presse
The Old American Can Factory
232 Third Street #E-303
Brooklyn, NY 11215
www.uglyducklingpresse.org

Distributed in the USA by SPD/Small Press Distribution
Distributed in Canada via Coach House Books by Raincoast Books
Distributed in the UK by Inpress Books

Cover design and typesetting by chuck kuan and goodutopian
Typeset in Times, Times Ten, Helvetica Neue, and Egyptienne
Printed and bound at McNaughton & Gunn
Covers printed letterpress at Ugly Duckling Presse
Inserts printed offset at Prestige Printing

This book has been made possible in part by the National Endowment for the Arts, the New York State Council on the Arts, by public funds from the New York City Department of Cultural Affairs in partnership with the City Council, and by the Community of Literary Magazines and Presses' Face Out program with support from the Jerome Foundation.

Chronology

Zahra Patterson

Chronology

"Seeing the small clean pink drops of memories. Tiny pink drops, like minute rubies, clung to the quartz of thoughts. Grazed my brain. And from deep down there my overarching yearning for a single glittering drop to sizzle the hot stony tongue. Language. Knotted tightly around my eyes like a bandage made of headaches. Language. Shards of a broken glued-together mirror. In it knotting my tie. English images came out of the barn with a thousand Zulus at my heels. She found me wedged tightly between past and present … I held my emotions tightly."

—Dambudzo Marechera, from *Black Sunlight*

maqakonako

from: Liepollo Rantekoa
to: Zahra Patterson
date: Jan 7 2011
subject: ...

titbit to say hello...
from the mountain kingdom. (echo)

love,
the self employed unemployable liepollo

p.s. the last statement in sesotho 'means'
one cannot buy a greeting...
also get a sesotho/english dictionary

from: Zahra Patterson
to: Liepollo Rantekoa
date: Dec 3 2014
subject: ...

I'm sorry I never replied to this my friend.

I'm going to read your work at an event[1] today.

miss you always.

Liepollo's "titbit" was an attached document. It was a commentary she'd recently written called "The Uncomfortable Gaze." (See Attachment I)[2]

I have also recently tried to get a dictionary, as you've instructed.

When I first searched Sesotho-English dictionaries, Northern Sotho-English dictionaries appeared in my search engine. So I did some research and quickly learned that there are three Sotho linguistic groups[3]: Northern Sotho, Southern Sotho, and Western Sotho, which is Setswana. Southern Sotho is the Sesotho of Lesotho, so I set off to find that dictionary.

> "In 1841 [a missionary from France], one of the three pioneers, Arbousset, Casalis, and Gossellin, of the Société des Missions Evangéliques de Paris, who reached Thaba Bosiu, Basutoland on 28th June, 1833, published in Paris his *Etudes sur la Langue Séchuana*. [A different missionary from France] considers this work to be a grammar of Southern Sotho and not Tswana, but of this [yet another French missionary] says, 'As a matter of fact, it is not easy to tell, on account of the spelling and the mixture of forms. Evidently it represents the dialect of the people round Thaba Nthšo, who were then, as they are now, BaTšwana (BaRolong), but whose language is much interspersed with Southern Sotho elements.'"[4]

I knew Sesotho and Setswana were close because I remember my Motswana cousin saying something along those lines to my Mosotho friend—even though they never met. Memory, like history, can be imaginary.

I went to South Africa to attend a wedding in Johannesburg. Then I traveled to Cape Town, where I met Liepollo. After a spell at Victoria Falls via Windhoek, the desert city where I was caught in an incredible, torrential downpour, I went to Gaborone, Botswana, to see my Motswana cousin. That was toward the end of my trip. Thus my memory is impossible, and the missionaries recklessly merged tongues.[5]

I haven't bought a Southern Sotho-English dictionary because the prices are prohibitive. I searched the NYPL and access is limited to on-site at research locations. I've decided that the libraries are my parameters—the control group—in my language acquisition experiment. I won't use the internet.

> "The SOUTHERN SOTHO Bible is the result of the labours of many men, no one name seeming to stand out ... After publishing a little catechism at the Cape in 1837, Casalis translated Mark and S. Rolland (who established Beer-séba Mission) John, which gospels were printed in 1839, as well as Seyo sa lipelu (Nourishment for the heart) a selection of fifty chapters from the Old and New Testaments, from the pen of Arbousset."[6]

In retrospect, there is something religious about the laws I laid. My heroic martyrdom for scholarship, like a missionary.

Liepollo,
I'm learning your language with dictionaries at the library:
bukantswe—dictionary.

Pronouns: Maemedi:

I - nna

you - wena

he/she - yena / yena
it - yona

we - re

you - o

they - ba

me - nna

you - wena

7

Glossary[8]

khetheli (lereho/noun)
Lerato la lapeng, le ikhethileng.
A special love for one's home.

kh'onaisa (lereho/noun)
Motho ea nang le tsebo e batsi le tatso e ikhethileng ka ntho e itseng.
An expert in a particular subject.

'mopuoa (lereho/noun)
Mong ea tsoang lefats'eng le leng ntle le leo re phelang ho lona.
A being from beyond planet Earth. An extraterrestrial.

maqakonako (lereho/noun)
Ketso kapa kabelo ea ho etela nako efeng kapa efeng lipakeng tsa bokhale le bokamoso.
The act/ability to travel to any time in the past and the future.

repolla (leetsi/verb)
Ho qholotsa botsmaisa u itlhalosa ka mokhoa o nonofetseng.
To challenge power through creative expression.

tlhacho-nko (lereho/noun)
Monko o u busetsang nakong tse fetileng tse hlabosang.
A smell that incites a sense of nostalgia.

repolla

Mendi + Keith Obadike @ The Met Breuer in collaboration with Vijay Iyer: Relation

Mendi and Keith sit at a table and their audience is on three sides. The room is dark. The performers are spotlighted. The audience, mostly white and some Asian, at least 3 black, exits and enters like silhouettes during the 30-minute set.

I'm listening to a discomfortable performance of numbers that represent people who were lynched by mobs of hate. Mendi and Keith speak in turn, methodically reciting single digits, to a soundtrack of higher and lower frequencies. I think about the density and complexity of the relationship between law and retribution

the systemic criminality against black bodies

Who are the people behind the numbers
resonating holocaust
Maafa

Where is the record of the dates and names of all the murdered Africans

How many were abducted from their families
Tortured to death
Murdered

Who died in the Maafa
on foreign soil
in bondage

Severed from our languages.

from: Liepollo Rantekoa
bcc: Zahra Patterson
date: Feb 23 2011
subject: PRESS RELEASE: Ba re e nere…Litfest Lesotho (March 2011)

FOR IMMEDIATE RELEASE

Ba re e nere...Litfest Lesotho (March 2011)

"The only thing that was certain was the realization that the act of writing was a supreme effort at finding your way through immense confusion. It is the act of 'finding your way' through a turbulent sea of words. The only thing that sustains you is a daring act of faith. You'll get somewhere. Somehow, I did."
– *from Njabulo Ndebele's "Iph'indlela," Steve Biko Memorial Lecture, September 2000*

Literature is an ongoing conversation that engages a politics of friendship; a process of discussion and discovery that takes place across multiple platforms and in various spaces and contexts. Literature also cannot be confined to a provincial way of relating to, expressing, narrating and even acknowledging it. The role of extra-textual references also cannot be ignored when engaging in literary discourse. The *Ba re e nere...*Litfest (March 2011) seeks to encourage discourse on these factors. Throughout the month of March 2011, *Ba re e nere...*Litfest (March 2011) will pay homage to literatis by exploring their work and experiences through the access to *Chimurenga Library* at the Vodacom Internet Shop (Maseru, Lesotho), screening of audio-visual material as well as the hosting of weekly discussions throughout the month of March 2011 in Lesotho.

See attachment for more info.

(See Attachment II)

from: Liepollo Rantekoa
to: Zahra Patterson
date: May 20 2011
subject: thoughts and or suggestions?

love and lite!

from: Zahra Patterson
to: Liepollo Rantekoa
date: May 24 2011
subject: thoughts and or suggestions?

I think it looks great.
is it a flyer for an event or just a great image?
what's your level of involvement with ba re literature?

from: Liepollo Rantekoa
to: Zahra Patterson
date: May 25 2011
subject: thoughts and or suggestions?

thanx for looking at it choma!!! it is a review—one where the reviewer is not only the frame but involved because that is what a reviewer does.
i am the founder, conceptualizer and curator of ba re ... it is me baby!

how goes raw fiction? am admiring the questions you posing to yourself ... i need to dig deeper in that aspect with ba re...

There were two attachments in the email. A Word document and an image:

This is the cover art of Lesego Rampolokeng's *Bantu Ghost: A stream of (black) unconsciousness*. At the time, I must have assumed it was publicity for Ba re e ne re, which it may have also been. The Word document included an excerpt of Rampolokeng's *Bantu Ghost* and a review by Liepollo. (See Attachment III)

March 11, 2015

My dear Liepollo,

Ba re e nere Literary Festival lives on! Someone is keeping your concept alive. They are publishing writers from Lesotho in an online competition, and the first story published on the new website is in Sesotho.

You always wanted me to learn your language, so I've decided to (attempt to) translate this story:

"Bophelo bo naka li maripa" by Lits'oanelo Yvonne Nei[9]

> "U tla llela metsotso ngoan'ake, ke bona u potlakile haholo." Ke mantsoe a nkhono ao, homme a sa hlokofala hee mofokeng eo ke ketso tsaka tsa bocheng. E se feela, nkile ka nkuoa ke lefatše ke tletsoe ke boikhantšo, ke lumela hore ha ho poho-peli, poho ke 'na feela! Ke ne ke holisoa ke eena nkhono ke le ntho e ka matsohong ke sa hloke letho, empa ea re ha ke kena boroetsaneng ka fetoha tuu ka makatsa ba bangata ba neng ba ntšepile...

Question Words: Mantswe a botsang:

How? - Jwang?

Why? - Hobaneng?

When? - Neng?

What? - Eng?

Where - Hokae?

Who - Mang?

Which - Efe?

Prepositions: Mahokedi:

about - ka
above - ka hodimo
across - ka nqane
after - ka mora
against - kgahlanong / mabapi le
along - ithatikile
around - ho potoloha
at - ho
back - morao
before - pele
behind - ka mora
below - ka tlasa
beneath - ka tlase
beside - ka thoko ho
between - mahareng
by - ka

down - tlase
for - ho etsetsa
from - ho tswa ho
in - ka hare
inside - ka hara
front - ka pele
near - haufi
next - pela
of - ya
off - ho tlohela
out - ntle
outside - ka ntle
over - ka hodima
since - ho tloha
through - ho phunyeletsa/ka
till - ho fihlela
to - ho
toward - ho isa / ho ya ho

March 31, 2015

"She's dead," I said out loud. I hadn't meant to say it that way. Cold and abrupt. Untrue.

Revelations:

The translation itself is arbitrary; what is important is my interaction with her language.

The form is unlikely to be straightforward. I'm envisioning a narrative structure resembling *Dictee* but I am unsure so much as yet to how, and other possibilities have appeared to me.

There are old emails—between me and Liepollo (dee-eh-PO-lo)—that will probably find their way into this manuscript.

The act of translation might also become less arbitrary.

´mopuoa

10 December 2009—En route to Cape Town
Reading Zakes Mda. *The Whale Caller* (2005)

"Hair. It is a blight they must carry on their heads, exposing
the position each head occupied in the statutory hierarchies
of the past. The troubles of humanity are locked in the
hair. Yet the people have managed to disguise their shame
by painting it in the colors that designate them all a people
of the rainbow. Without exception. Without a past. Without
rancour. Without hierarchies. Only their eyes betray the
big lie. In these eyes you can see a people living in a
daze. Rainbow people walking in a precarious dream
that may explode into a nightmare without much warning."

It was in Johannesburg, in Melville, "a real neighborhood" I declared in my notebook—having spent my first two days in Jozi in high-security luxury estates. Bafana, the Zimbabwean driver who told stories about teasing crocodiles in the Zambezi as a boy and always carried change in his dashboard to give away, had dropped me off. I walked down a block to a couple of bookshops that faced each other. I chose the old-school-looking shop. A black woman, not the owner, stood behind the counter, and I was her only customer. After a few confused minutes, I approached her and asked for black writers. She frowned slightly and said there were none in the shop. She offered me a collection of shorts by Nadine Gordimer and a novel by Alan Paton. I purchased the stories, and crossed the street to find black South African writers in the other shop that I determined was owned by gay white men. This is where I bought Mda's *The Whale Caller*, which I read on a 28-hour economy-class train ride.

NOTES [MARACHERA]

(1) SCRAPIAN BLUES

(2) HOUSE OF HUNGER

* MENIPPEAN NOVEL

liepollor@gmail.com

I'd been in Cape Town for a little over a week when we met.

She entered to use the waiter's mobile. Then asked to put her bags at my table for safekeeping while she ran down the block to buy him minutes. She didn't know him. She didn't know me. She commanded the space with her tiny presence.

Upon her return, she noticed a book on my table and demanded to know why I was—who indeed I was to be—reading Dambudzo Marechera's *Black Sunlight*. She then gave me a list of her favorite titles on a piece of notepaper, along with her email address.

Our first encounter was brief, but I emailed her the next day or so.

from: Zahra Patterson
to: Liepollo Rantekoa
date: Dec 19 2009
subject: Black Sunlight at Lola's

Hi Liepollo,

I don't have a phone number or anything, so I'm hard to contact. Will be in town until mid-January ... i think ... the hostel is expensive ... know anyone looking for an extra thousand-ish rand for a couch until Jan 15th? ...this is a different country from the US, sublets are a way of life there. But yes, I'm not looking for a travel agent. Would love to meet up sometime this week. I have no plans, so you name a time and a place and that's perfect.

see you later,
Zahra

from: Liepollo Rantekoa
to: Zahra Patterson
date: Dec 21 2009
subject: Black Sunlight at Lola's

Hey Zahra,

i knew the was a reason why i was all up in your face (my apologies but when I marachera is being read then i see stars)! i am actually currently looking for someone to rent my room (and sleep on a couch) ... PLUS the way my bills are, i am definitely looking for an extra thousand-ish.

umm, i guess email is the communique way e.g. when or if you would like to see the place...
i live in 4B Bedford Road, Observatory....ssooo if you get this email before 5pm, you can view it today (as i am home until then) or we can plan for tomorrow....we can discuss figas when we meet.

hetep,
Liepollo

from: Liepollo Rantekoa
to: Zahra Patterson
date: Dec 21 2009
subject: Black Sunlight at Lola's

today, being (21 december)...

from: Liepollo Rantekoa
to: Zahra Patterson
date: Dec 22 2009
subject: Black Sunlight at Lola's

ola, congrats on finding the place!
great news! I am at home the whole day today (words are not coming as fast as i had hoped, so now i have to sweet talk my pen … found so much to do in the house in lieu of getting a eureka moment).
so pop by and we will take it from there—you can supply the money later today when you move in.

i am getting a friends mattress on wednesday, so you can take my room for tonite and i will sleep in my house mates room.

till then is now, black light
liep
p.s. thanx!!!

from: Zahra Patterson
to: Liepollo Rantekoa
date: Dec 24 2009
subject: Black Sunlight at Lola's

oh i should have left a note to say i won't be back tonight.
hope you're feeling better.
the key works great, i'm so happy.
see you later roomie.

from: Liepollo Rantekoa
to: Zahra Patterson
date: Dec 24 2009
subject: Black Sunlight at Lola's

a few hours later and i is a-l-i-v-e … till then is know,
greatness
sharp,
liep

tlhacho-nko

"Making this book is a strange thing to me: in Sesotho we say mohlolo—a miracle, or a wonder. Most of the people in my life—my family, my friends, my neighbours—most of them cannot read. Almost none of them can read English ... I have worked at the University cleaning houses since 1968. It is at the University that I meet Limakatso, I call her motsoalle oa ka, my very good friend. I tell her my stories and she writes them down in a computer to make them a book. Mohlolo!"[10]

One of the chapters in Nthunya's autobiography that impresses me is "When a Woman Loves a Woman." She tells the story of a friendship between her and another woman. "It's like when a man chooses you for a wife, except when a man chooses, it's because he wants to share the blankets with you. The woman chooses you the same way, but she doesn't want to share the blankets. She wants love only. When a woman loves another woman, you see, she can love her with a whole heart."[11] The two women celebrate their friendship, attend church together, and share food when times are hard. I think of Liepollo and her cultural context, and my cultural context, and our shared/separate contemporary Cape Town context of traveler and resident.

I found *Singing Away the Hunger: The Autobiography of an African Woman* at the Brooklyn Public Library. Mpho 'M'atsepo Nthunya, a polyglot and natural storyteller, thought her stories in Sesotho while translating them into English as she spoke them to her editor, K. Limakatso Kendall, who transcribed them as they were spoken.

"When they had settled on the written version of the individual stories, Kendall gave them a more or less chronological order, as it seemed most rational to her. This aspect of the narrative did not concern Nthunya herself, and the apparent absense of teleology (Cribb 2003), or plot, from her approach to gathered life-stories—individual tales are strongly plotted—implies that her oral culture has given her a rather different view from the life-as-development model used by Kendall. Nthunya's sense of how her life-stories might be organised is never stated, but I assume it is likely to derive from praise poetry and its influence on oral prose narrative. '...the spirit of the story is more important than the plot...' (Coplan 1987, 12)" (Daymond 97).

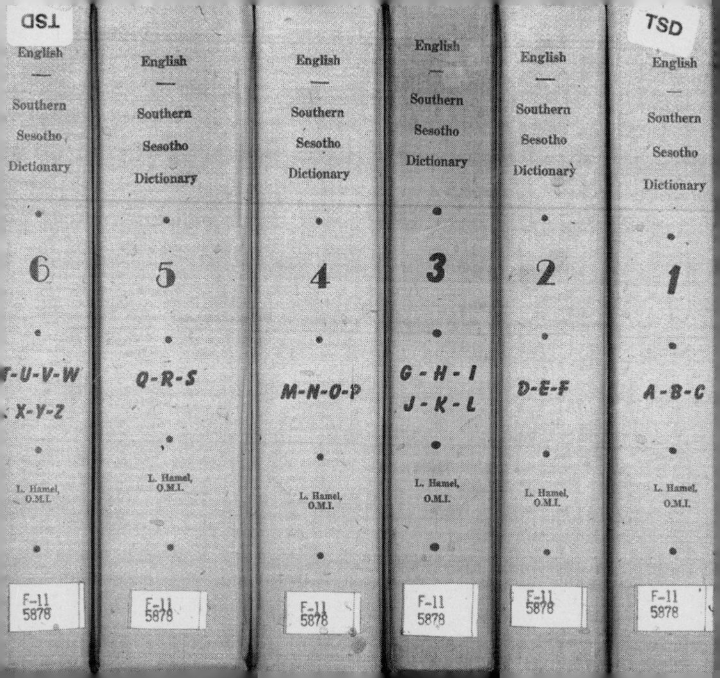

English — Southern Sesotho Dictionary

6

T-U-V-W
X-Y-Z

L. Hamel, O.M.I.

English — Southern Sesotho Dictionary

5

Q-R-S

L. Hamel, O.M.I.

English — Southern Sesotho Dictionary

4

M-N-O-P

L. Hamel, O.M.I.

English — Southern Sesotho Dictionary

3

G-H-I
J-K-L

L. Hamel, O.M.I.

English — Southern Sesotho Dictionary

2

D-E-F

L. Hamel, O.M.I.

English — Southern Sesotho Dictionary

1

A-B-C

L. Hamel, O.M.I.

Choma,

It's Friday. Raining. April 10.

A lover asked about my tattoo and I told her about you. I wonder, if you were alive, would I have told her about you? Would I be telling you about her?

I am at the Science, Industry and Business Library. I had requested a six-volume set of dictionaries to help me get your language into mine, as I attempt to translate Yvonne Nei's short story. However, it is a one-way dictionary. For English speakers only. There is no Southern Sesotho into English section.

This is frustrating because I have wasted my time in coming here, to this library. It is frustrating politically, too.

Love,
Zahra

September 25, 2012: I was sitting behind the front desk at Doctors Without Borders USA scrolling through Facebook when I noticed one of Liepollo's colleagues at Chimurenga had changed his profile picture to an image of her. My stomach dropped and I sent him a one-line inquiry hoping for an inane explanation. I went home early that day. The next day, after work, I walked into a tattoo parlor around the corner and had ke nonyana—the first words I spoke in Sesotho—inked onto my arm so no future day could pass without memory.

Translation of April 10 letter using the six-volume, one-way dictionary:

Mōkanē,

Ke labōhlanō. Khanyapa(li)/pula(li)/takōtso(li).

April: n: 'mesa; mphe—ke-khōtŝe; mōramang; Mōputlò

Lover :n : morati(ba); serati(li); babonyetsani; bafèrèhani; baratani; mōrata(ba)
Love-making :n :lērèrèhi(ma)

Memory :n: kèlèllo(li); pelo-mahopotsane(pl); mohopolo(mē); khōpōlō(li); kelèllo ea litaba tse fetileng

To escape from one's memory: ho khohl-a(ile)

Library :n : pōkello-ea-libuka; ntlō ea libuka; mabukeng; polokelo-ea-libuka

English: n: chomi(mine slang); lenyesemane(ma)

Dictionary: n: bukantsoe; bukantsu (N.S.); pukantsu (N.S.); buka eo ho ngotsoeng ho eona mantsoe le hlaloso ea 'ona kappa le photolelo ea 'ona puong e sele

Love (to)v: ho rat-a(ile);tt: ho ratè-la(tsē)

rata,
your choma

The most difficult access point at the beginning of this process was not having a grammar handbook to pair with the vocabulary. In the above translation, I attempted to simulate the disjointed experience of reading the dictionary, the strange spacing, and the multiple unexplained words. N.S. we might assume is Northern Sotho. Ba is plural for Mo; and I can only guess what the other terms in parentheses are, masculine and feminine perhaps.

Dec. 4th 2009—Soweto Township
(Driving tour, Regina Mundi Church, Apartheid Museum)

Tonight is my second night in Johannesburg. Just my cousin and my uncle in the executive suite apartment for dinner. He spoke and my cousin, Y, and I interspersed with questions. It started with him asking if my sister, X, was the only one married. I told him both U and I were gay. He was surprised. I don't look like a lesbian. Y didn't catch what he'd said, her father, who'd left her as an infant in Cuba, where she was born, as he fled to Liberia. Algeria. Paris. Nigeria. Khartoum. I repeated his words matter of factly. She laughed. She has a great laugh.

I learned all about homosexuality in Africa. Rampant in Arabs. Everyone in Liberia's elite: they marry, man to woman, both gay. It is not a discussion in Africa. The last thing the continent needs to deal with is a gay rights movement. In northern Nigeria, boys and girls are kept apart. All the boys in their boarding schools are fags. Their teachers predators. It is not a discussion.

He is hard to follow sometimes, my uncle. He was friends with Baldwin. Tight … Pauses. Not like Gillespie, filling all the space. Poetry. My uncle. My father's brother. My big father started to sing a poem he wrote in '85. He no longer writes poetry. Did the most, his best, in Paris, '71. After leaving the Party. Y asks what his major regret/letdown was with the Party. He sits down in the armchair. The Black Panthers. He speaks of them with their first names. Eldridge. Stokely. New York men I've never heard of.

They were destined to arrive. In the wake of Malcolm X. Destined to fail—drugged up, arrogant public drinkers in leather trench coats. Huey would take party money to gamble in Nevada. Electric shock treatment in prisons. There was a rift in the party. New York wanted to kill them. My uncle convinced them not to. Cleaver was speed. Newton cocaine. Carmichael weed. Cleaver hated Baldwin. Was not a threat, his *Soul on Ice*, because it doesn't penetrate. He does not look inside: rapist, wife-beater. His wife, Kathleen, was like a sister to my uncle.

An eleven-year-old boy was gunned down by New York City police in a Brooklyn housing project ... There was a vision to hold trials and keep records of the sentences. To publish the notes...[12]

He is funny, my uncle, who does not want to see gay tactics—antics—in the late-sixties as he gets off the IRT in the West Village, but wants free consciousness. Doesn't want to see queerness flaunted, just wants people to be. My uncle who carried a six-shooter under his long suit jacket and threatened cops when he saw them beating black men; he draws a line at flamboyance.

Free consciousness, I smile. Uncle, you are an idealist. He does not like that. We are at the dinner table discussing gays. He speaks of Baldwin's suffering and analyzes his own gay brother.

For Africa, he concedes, perhaps he is an idealist.

Sunday.

And the scramble for Africa continues. Solar power. Tour guides. Companies. Being irresponsible and hiring externally. Not funding internal training programs.

I've walked to the top of Longmarket Street. Found a view of mountains and ocean. Can see the spread of city. Center with mild skyscrapers—in quantity and height. The port. Glistening blue water and a spotless sky.

At this point in my journal, I had stopped noting the date. It is mid-December, 2009.

I could have gone to Malawi and stayed out of debt. But I had to come to Cape Town to find who I am. This city is me: the separate coexistence of Europe and Africa. Yet I am one. And it is one. The separation is part of the whole. What completes the essence is the unbearable dichotomy within. Yet we bear it, don't we. The Monster—the oppressed. The Fool—the oppressor. And vice-versa. And within all us western-ethnic folk, we carry and cope with this dichotomy. When you become your own monster's fool, you will have achieved self-awareness. Then you can live with your dual self.

"You will never be a woman unless your womb is full," Saed told me. I met him at the entrance to a cemetery. Curiosity had led me there. The above quote came a little less than halfway through our conversation.

His eyes were grayish blue. A sweet soul who has lived too much. The whites reddened with age. Rheumy or getting there. A button-down blue shirt. Suspenders. And a baseball cap. We exchanged pleasantries. He told me about the cemetery. People who were exiled on Robben Island way long ago are bones on this precipice...

He asked if I was religious. [He was Muslim.] I told him the truth: I do not need to know what is unknown. I do not believe nor am I a nonbeliever. He stood, offered me his seat. I did not sit. He insisted. I refused.

I told him I respected what he believed and I would not want to change his mind. He told me he just wanted to tell me the truth. He did not want to change my mind.

"A woman is useless to herself unless she has a baby. The meaning of life is love and creating a human with that love."

Robben Island was used as a prison since early colonization, but it's likely Saed was referring to the lepers who were sent/imprisoned there in the late 19th century.

How did he know I was searching for meaning? Well, I am off the tourist track engaged in a conversation with an old man.

My only resistance is to sitting through a lecture. I insist on speaking, too.

The Quran. The Bible. He knows these books well. They are history. Truth. I had to disagree.

There was something special about this South African of Asian descent who has lived through much. Even though he wanted to simply lecture he was also able to hear. He did not disagree that history is skewed or biased and thus not truth.

As humans there cannot be a set truth but only an individual's or a society's. Depending.

I liked his eyes. His soul. He told me he was too old for me. I would kill him. It could never be. But maybe I was wishing he were younger. I laughed. Heartily. He hit my arm. Was pleased.

Sometimes he came so close our eyes locked. My black open to his pale green. He could see I wanted no man. My words told him I did not feel the need to find love or give birth. But, yes, it would be nice, I confessed.

I corrected him when he said we came from sperm. That the womb, woman, was so important because she gave birth to men.

He liked my modern mind. My feminism. It tickled him. My compulsion to push language toward inclusivity.

No matter how educated we become, we do not fulfill our purpose on this planet unless we make life from love. A beautiful thought. I wish all life did come from love.

Tuesday.

"...Hurriedly I took off my priest's garb. Dressed. Grabbed the cameras and raced for my car. I drove with ease. Parked. And waited. This tyranny of WAITING. It should be blown right out of people's lives. The fucking stinking waiting. At bus stops, railway stations, subways, traffic lights, shop counters, toilets, at the undertakers. At. At. At." p. 109 (Ch. 9)

Last day at the hostel ... Pangs of E this morning.

A whole world of difference. Now. Reading Marechera. Living in Cape Town. Friends with a Xhosa man. A man from Malawi. A woman from Germany. A woman from Lesotho. Soon to room with a woman from Namibia.

"And I dismantle myself into an overnight suitcase where I last all winter like a premonition." p. 113 (Ch. 10), Marechera.

Almost finished reading. But listening to Europeans talking about buying cheap African property is disturbing. I'm almost gone...

24th Dec. 2009. Thursday.

Yesterday was chapter 2 and we ended up in each other's arms. Dancing. Climbing narrow stairs with three glasses of water. Dominos with no introductions. A bed in another room. A bottle of the Wandering Grape. Artsy atmosphere. Young people. Old barman. The coolest cat there. Quality tunes. Low lighting. Remembering red walls. Back home with chips. Dancing. Smoking across the threshold. Turning. Jazzing and jiving. Then I gave her water and said goodnight...

25th Dec. Merry Christmas hangover. Drinking Tsingtao and water watching sports. Football. Familyless. Friendless. Solo Christmas under a warm blue sky ... Around 1 o'clock I would guess.

I wonder what chapter 3 will bring. More imagination. More giggles. More cuddles. At an Asian restaurant. Hip hop playing lightly. Louder music on the street. I took the metro free today. Gave a blind guitarist a rand. Ignored man next to me who tried to ponder how much 'those guys' make a day...

Chapter 3 starts with me coming home. The key isn't working again. She comes to the door. Opens it. Goes back to bed. My bed. Her bed. I'd been out all night. I went into the bathroom and cut off all my hair. She continues sleeping. It must be 3 or 4 in the afternoon. A dirty, tri-colored stocking hangs at the fireplace. A note reads "...YOU KNOW THE REST."

The last chapter ended ambiguously. We were too drunk. Dancing to LPs. A flirtation arose. Or I became aware of it. Perhaps I wasn't getting something when she was calling me a beautiful person. And then she wanted to sleep in my arms. I'm not sure if going to sleep ended the chapter or if the morning after, waking up alone, preparing an excellent breakfast and neither of us mentioning anything was the actual end of chapter. Me leaving without saying goodbye because she'd gone back to bed. Actually it might work out, having only one bed. I sleep at night and she through the day.

Being neat and tidy / Ukuba linono kanye nokuzithanda / Ho ba makgethe le ho hlweka

Sunday. Chapter 84. The Musical at Kalk Bay. Chapter 21. Losing the Wallet. Again.

> Ke nonyana. I'm a bird.
> Kea leboha, tanki!

12-30

"One must know that the soul is unaffected and unchanged by the ups and downs which are experienced by the ego-personality." From "The Philosophy of Sleep and The Four States of Consciousness." *Egyptian Yoga: The Philosophy of Enlightenment*. By Sebai Dr. Muata Ashby

"Buddha emphasized attaining salvation rather than asking so many questions."

Nirvana
Right Understanding
Right Thought
Right Speech
Right Action
Right Meditation
Right Mindfulness
Right Effort
Right Livlihood

"The Saturday and Sundays of Alexandra roar, groan and rumble, like a troubled stomach. The same days in Johannesburg are as silent as the stomach of a dead person." from Ch. 3. To Every Birth its Blood. © 1981. Mongane Serote

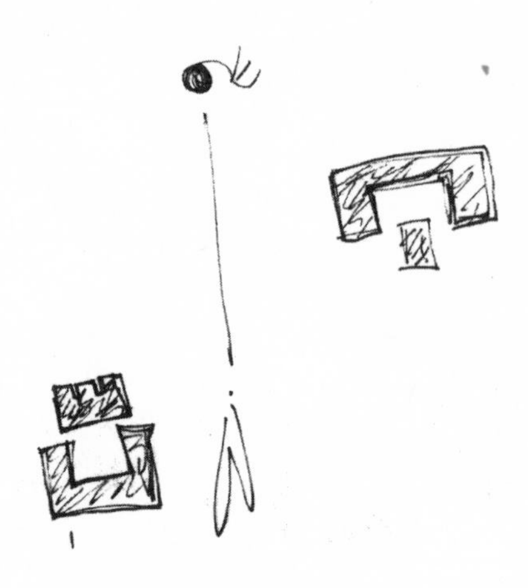

[And a drawing that Liepollo must have made in my journal.]

Translation of April 10 translated letter:

mōkanē
ke nonyana, kèlèllo
a turntable after wine
at Tagore's
turning, you, we, turning
lērèrèhi
lērèrèhi
ke nonyana, i said
bukantsoe, you said

before we met
j'y suis allé
polokelo-ea-libuka

after we met
ho rat-a
unexplored
put aside for the future
ho khohl-a
ke morati, bamōrata

kh'onaisa

"Indeed, language is so overwhelmingly oral that of all the many thousands of languages—possibly tens of thousands—spoken in the course of human history, only around 106 have ever been committed to writing to a degree sufficient to have produced literature, and most have never been written at all. Of the some 3000 languages spoken that exist today only some 78 have a literature (Edmonson 1971). There is as yet no way to calculate how many languages have disappeared or been transmuted into other languages before writing came along. Even now hundreds of languages in active use are never written at all: no one has worked out an effective way to write them. The basic orality of language is permanent."[13]

Bronx Museum of Art | Thursday, May 7, 2015 | 6:30–8:30pm
"The Witnesses: What is the value of age and wisdom?"

Vinie Burrows, Boubacar Boris Diop, Yusef Komunyakaa, Achille Mbembe, Ngũgĩ wa Thiong'o.
Moderated by Rashidah Ismaili

The room is white walls with windows onlooking the green-leafed trees of Grand Concourse. Alive with a buzz of literary-type voices. A clear plastic podium stands next to two folding tables covered by black tablecloths. Five microphones deck the tables, each with a de-branded, short bottle of water next to it. Five black chairs sit empty, waiting for the panelists.

Rashidah Ismaili enters and invites the writers to their chairs, in alphabetical order. Burrows sits in the chair closest to the podium.

RASHIDAH: As is traditional in Africa, each will be introduced in turn and speak a few words. Then we will have a discussion.

Vinie reads an excerpt of Boubacar's work, translated into English from French or Wolof.

BOUBACAR: A Wolof saying, a French saying … it is important to listen to elders.

Vinie reads a Komunyakaa poem.

YUSEF: A portable internalized landscape … the ghosts, the living, the dead converge within the psyche … the raconteurs sipping nostalgia and moonshine … how would we know happiness if sorrow or grief veered away.

Vinie reads from "Time on the Move."

ACHILLE: Mzee Ngũgĩ, the eldest. (*Laughter.*) The question posed for us to respond to today was to share some reflections on the value of age, wisdom, and witnessing … What is it, to be called on to testify … the witness speaks on behalf of justice and life; the pursuit of truth is the key to justice.

Vinie reads from The River Between.

NGŨGĨ: Education can take away from the mind of the recipient … the spirit goes to exile: the spirit of a culture lies in language. The problem of Africa: they give their accents and we give them access.

RASHIDAH: What are some of the ways you write in response to the world?

YUSEF: Write everything down, read everything aloud. No topic is taboo. Beauty is always part of the telling … There is a tension between the scientific and artistic.

BOUBACAR: The Rwandan genocide in 1994. Changed my life, my way of writing. A writer cannot talk of suffering from far away.

RASHIDAH: How does a writer deal with the charge of witnessing?

ACHILLE: Before you speak, there is a coercive framework ready to interpret, to trap, meaning. If the language we use is in itself a prison … We have to put a bomb under the language. Explode language!

RASHIDAH: What and who inspires you?

NGŨGĨ: Fanon. He gave us the vocabulary to understand the historical moment. Read Fanon everyday.

BOUBACAR: Cheik Hamidou Kane. Seek cultural level before economic. Decolonize the mind before tending to politics.

RASHIDAH: Last words. Two minutes each. There was a miscommunication between PEN [American Center] and the Museum. We have to wrap up quickly.

NGŨGĨ: Help young people access their resources.

ACHILLE: Racism is being recycled in old and new forms. Fate of Africa is the fate of the diaspora.

YUSEF: The colonization of the heart. Whenever the heart is colonized, the dance has ended.

BOUBACAR: Slavery was a crime against humanity. Teaching Wolof enhances self-esteem. Our own realities.

◆ ◆ ◆

I first read Ngũgĩ in 2005. I was twenty-three and in Africa for the first time. I spent two months in Kenya, and only read Kenyan writers. I fell in love with a little play called *The Trial of Dedan Kimathi*, about the leader of the Mau Mau.

In South Africa, I read Zakes Mda, Mongane Serote, Bessie Head, and, of course, Dambudzo Marechera. I went to Johannesburg for a wedding, and stayed as a tourist. I wanted to exist outside the international development crowd. I took the train to Cape Town and found Marechera. I was enjoying a leisurely lunch on Long Street reading *Black Sunlight* and editing my novel, and I met Liepollo.

"[In 1952, the] Mau Mau or the Kenya Land and Freedom Army ... ushered in the era of modern guerilla warfare in Africa" (*Decolonising the Mind* 24).

"With independence ... there was a gradual revolt although it was still largely confined to the four walls of the school, the social hall, the university premises, and also to the boundaries of the English language. ...The revolt took many forms: one was the sheer African petty-bourgeois assertion in the very fact of writing and directing and performing plays. It also took the form of a more and more nationalistic patriotic and anti-neocolonial, anti-imperialist content in the plays, this trend perhaps best exemplified in Mĩcere Mũgo's and Ngũgĩ wa Thiong'o's *The Trial of Dedan Kimathi* which was performed by the Kenya Festac 77 Drama Group" (39).

August 4, 2015

Choma,

I'm revisiting this manuscript in which I speak to your memory, to your language. One thing I thought to do was to revisit the conversation I created with stolen words noted during the panel "The Witnesses." There must have been a problem with the recording of the event because it is not to be found among the other event recordings and video. I cannot return to the source to improve my memory. The event is in the past—thus incomplete. I write to you, again. While listening to a recording of another event from the same festival: "Queer Futures,"[14] featuring Binyavanga Wainaina, Zanele Muholi, and Kehinde Bademosi, *Chimurenga*[15] is mentioned and silence is the first topic of discussion.

Remember the day I picked you up from Chimurenga? You were dressed like Peter Pan and smoking a cigarette in the office. You hadn't come home the night before and were going out with some friends. I went along. After dinner we went to the beach and homosexuality, as a topic, came up. I tried to engage but walked away from your friends to watch the water splash the dark night shore in a safe solitude.

Silence as survival is no longer survival, says the moderator Shireen Hassim.

KB: Black gay men are still not visible in America.

ZM: Visibility basically means that people need to be able to read and write and visualize their daily experiences. Right now we don't have enough queer content that speaks to the Africans in their own languages. I don't know, why do people think that we have to write in English? … I'm a Zulu-speaking person, and when you go to Zimbabwe there are Shona people, there are Ndebele people, and if we were to use those languages we would be challenging our family members who think we're adopting "this thing" from the West. So there's a need to write queer terms, terminology, in our own vernac.

KB: Who tells the story controls the language. This language is the language of oppressors and this is a language against women.

BW, *speaking at a different event during the same festival*:[16] In 2050, all the globe will be inside fully the politics of Audre Lorde and James Baldwin, we will carry everybody in their love …

I wonder, often, what next steps your festival would have taken under your ever-evolving political eye.

your comrade in the struggle,

z

I found this in a Google search.

Bwesigye
@bwesigye
Follow

Liepollo Rantekoa died at 29. Tupac Shakur at 25. Hillary Kuteisa at 23. But their ideas live. Their ideas should live. #YouthDeaths

6:13 PM - 25 Dec 2015

khetheli

If all these rich South Africans were taxed off their asses it would make strides. Schools could be built in a minute. 20 years so much could be turned around. It is not yet dark. I am very tired.

"To write as though only one kind of reality subsists in the world is to act out a mentally retarded mime, for a mentally deficient audience." – p. 79, Black Sunlight

On Peasants and workers:

"... . They are not fighting for new needs, new ideas, new wants, but for what such people have always fought for. And lost. They are not really fighting. It is merely the whole society writhing as it were with indigestion or perhaps malnutrition. All they want is for the lioness to relent a little, give them a bit more rope. What they should do is kill her."

"'What about the workers and the peasants? Are you for them or against them? … because right now there are strikes, riots, demonstrations, bombings, and all to do with this question of transforming the nature of available reality.'

He smiled.

'More a question of transforming inequalities and salaries and housing and schools and hospitals I would think. More a question of extending to the available limit the freedoms that exist now … They are not fighting for new needs, new ideas, but for what such people have always fought for. And lost'" (Marechera 79).

Marechera's narrator-protagonist is having a conversation with his double in a nightmarish scene in which he arrives at a place called Devil's End. They are trapped in a violent postcolonial Kafkaesque hallucination. Postcolonial identity is present but it is not so different from the oppressed identity of peasants and workers anywhere. Fighting for what they have always fought for, and lost. "The work of Dambudzo Marechera stands out as a unique expression of self and postcolonial identity … His fiction … undermines any fixed notions of a unified and stable 'self' or 'history.' Additionally, the postsructuralist and deconstructive elements within his work put pressure on the construction of meaning at the level of language and narrative" (Buuck 118). The urgency of now against the backdrop of always. It is particularly unsettling to reencounter this work—his work and my work, this manuscript—in August 2017, as the world is literally drowning in the shit it created. "So we think of Prometheus as the first man to not only read his shit but also to suffocate in it" (Marechera 63).

April 23, 2015

Choma,

Access to your language is limited.

I am at the Schomburg Center for Research in Black Culture, it's part of the New York Public Library system. I was hoping to teach myself some grammar today, yet I have another dictionary that isn't helpful.

Remember our guerilla plan to cover all the heads of statues of evil white dictators with giant sacks?

I miss you.

zahra

Cheers and protests as University of Cape Town removes Cecil Rhodes statue

Large crowds watch figure of colonial-era magnate taken away from campus, despite opposition from Afrikaner solidarity group

Agence France-Presse in Cape Town | Thursday 9 April 2015

Black students have celebrated the fall of a statue of British colonialist Cecil Rhodes at the University of Cape Town, as some white groups protested at what they see as threats to their heritage.

Cheers went up as a crane removed the bronze statue from its plinth at South Africa's oldest university after a month of student demonstrations against a perceived symbol of historical white oppression.

Some students in the crowd of hundreds slapped the statue as it came down amid ululating and cries of "amandla" (power), while others splashed red paint on it and wrapped Rhodes's head in paper.[17]

South Africa is in harmony with a post-Charlottesville America. It is a bit surprising to see the starkness of black and white in the above article. In the United States, while whites have often been the perpetrators of heinous racist crimes, white people have always stood and died for racial justice, from John Brown to Heather Heyer.

We wanted those statues to be held accountable

I don't remember details of our conversations. But we were always talking art and revolution

with your roommate and her boyfriend

A Letter to The Mayor of Cape Town
cc: President Zuma; The Minister of Education; etc...

Dear Ms or Mr Mayor,

I have spent the last five weeks in the magnificent city of Cape Town. I wandered many neighborhoods, beaches, sections of Table Mountain National Park—climbed up Skeleton Gorge and down Platteklip Gorge—dined and drank in many a fine establishment, frequented bookshops and libraries, and fell in love with the Company's Garden in the city center.

One of my first days out and about as a tourist in Cape Town I went to the National Gallery. As *Lonely Planet* says, the permanent collection is rather dull, but the two temporary exhibits were fantastic. One was about the four Nobel Peace Prize winners of South Africa. Very well done. And then it flowed nicely from talented political South African artists to the madness of Dada.

Upon exiting, feeling intellectually fulfilled, marveling at the accessible entry fee of R15 (however strongly believing museums should be free), I noticed a giant statue of Jan Smuts.[18] The bastard. But there was a sack over his head.[19] Tied with rope. I thought, What a great idea! The statues standing mighty as the day they were erected are giving homage to the evil Boers. But a bag on the head, now that's relevant!

And then I found another statue. The bastard Cecil "Imperialist" Rhodes. Ick! Yuck. What the fuck is he doing here? Being commemorated. I'd like to see a bag on his head and a plaque in his hands with a formal apology and confirmation that he is drowning in the river Phlegethon in the seventh circle of Hell.

I'd like to see that on every statue. A sack of shame and a formal recognition of wrongdoing. An understanding of the violence of history. And it is not enough. I want revenge, not townships, reservations, and housing projects. I want 40 acres and a mule.

Why is the imperialist not ashamed? How can he and she look in the mirror every day? Why are they still so certain of their superiority? South Africa, you have not done enough! Your Boers should be on their knees, begging forgiveness. Your English need to pull the missionary sticks from their asses, get on their hands and knees and vomit the diamond money from their bowels back into the earth.

Why is education not free? Why are all the textbooks written from a white perspective? Why is the curriculum in township schools still just enough to get a job for the white man and follow his orders?

Oh, South Africa. You are so rich and so far behind. You should be ashamed.

Sincerely,
Zahra M.

P.S. Please wear the enclosed hemp sacks and secure with rope. There are no eyeholes. Soon enough there will be one for everyone in the world. I've already got mine.

September 25, 2015

The anniversary of your death and two days after your birthday.

I met your fiance today. He's the american guy from the peace corps who seemed so struck by your death on social media … I hadn't realized.

I brought the Betty Boop figurine you gave me and, for a few minutes, sat her awkwardly on the hotel bar.

He's the one who has continued *Ba re e ne re*. He's kept your project alive, with a writer from Lesotho.

We are the American missionaries for your cause.

He told me you weren't engaged, not officially. But you were planning on moving to D.C. to be with him. D.C.! I would have visited you.

We remembered how you would accuse us of working for *National Geographic* when we took your photo…

He told me you were killed by a reckless German driver: a volunteer in Lesotho. Yours was the only life lost. At 29. The driver was evacuated, forever unaccountable. The past is ever-present.

Language staccatos out, no flow to my feelings.

DIES (ONE WHO): n: mōshȯi(ba); mōtimeli(ba)

--at home: mō-shoela-habo;

--for others: mōsheeli(ba);

KILLED: v:

--by unknown people: ho soloa ke mothala; [20]

ka tla, ka bôna, ka tšea, I came, I saw, I took.

21

Empire then is empire now. Empire there is empire here.

Translation attempt 1[22]

“Bophelo bo naka li maripa” by Lits’oanelo Yvonne Nei

“U (*???*) tla (*come/will come*) llela (*weep for*) metsotso ngoan’ake, (*???*) ke (*I am*) bona (*look*) u (*?*) potlakile (*hurry?*) haholo” (*interjection hope*). Ke (*I am*) mantsoe (*black?*) a (*?*) nkhono (*up to now*) ao (*those … very same yonder*), homme (*?*) a (*?*) sa (*like/ dawn*) hlokofala (*become painful, be grieved*) hee (*exclamation of astonishment, disapproval*) mofokeng (*mofo—medicine or healer? keng—stranger*) eo (*that/those/it*) ke (*I am*) ketso (*?*) tsaka (*battle axe*) tsa (*their/they did*) bocheng (*?*). E (*?*) se (*?*) feela (*but, however, only, without reason*), nkile (*I once, I happened to*) ka (*past negative?*) nkuoa (*nku—sheep*) ke (*I am*) lefatše (*lefatsa—splinter, chip*) ke (*I am*) tletsoe (*tletse, of tlala- be full, of tlela—has come for*) ke (*I am*) boikhantšo (*boikgantsho—pride, self—exaltation, vaunting, arrogance, act of making a show of oneself*), ke (*I am*) lumela hore ha ho poho—peli (*??*), poho (*bull*) ke (*I am*) ‘na feela! (*but, however, only, without reason!*) Ke (*I am*) ne ke (*I am*) holisoa ke (*I am*) eena (*ee—yes, na—with*) nkhono (*up to now*) ke (*I am*) le ntho (*hair, strand, wire?*) e ka matsohong ke (*I am*) sa hloke letho (*something*), empa (*but*) ea (*yes*) re (*we, when, say/intend/do*) ha ke (*I am*) kena boroetsaneng (*boro-drill*) ka (*my/mine*) fetoha (*fetoga- become changed*) tuu (***go re tuu****—be silent, be quiet*) ka (*my/mine*) makatsa (*surprise*) ba bangata ba neng (*when;* ***e tla ba neng****—how long is it going to last?*) ba (*we*) ntšepile (*ntse—continued action; pile ... pila—good, well; piletsa—something that will bring evil*).

Translation of translation: Attempt 1

U will come weeping metsotso ngoan'ake,
I look u hurry hoping
I am black? up to now the same.
homme like dawn becomes painful, is grieved.
aie. no bueno.
The stranger is the healer those that I am ketso battle axe their bocheng.
E se however, not once you sheep,
I splinter, I am full, I am pride.
Ke lumela hore ha ho poho-peli,
bull I am 'na without reason.
Ke ne ke holisoa ke eena,
ee means yes, na is with,
up to now I have hair
e ka matsohong ke sa hloke something,
but yes we intend ha ke kena to
drill-etsaneng
changing silence, my surprise
ba bangata ba neng/when;
e tla ba neng how long is it going to last?
we continue to bring evil.

Translation of translation: Attempt 2

You came weeping
I am looking and hoping
Up to now those like dawn are grieved
I am at a loss, medicinal stranger
That I am a fighter
They bocheng. Without reason.
I splintered, full of arrogance
Hello, ha ho poho-peli,
Bull runs without reason
Yes your hair, yes something,
Yes we do drill
We have changed to silence
My surprise is our action to do good in the face of evil.

Translation of translation: Attempt 3

We weep for you who always were in a hurry
We grieve with sounds of sadness
Where was the medicine man
Will come like the magic warrior to heal you
Like the loss of our sheep,
There is no reason
The strangers took our pride,
Our bulls, their arrogance
We stand on a wire,
Precarious as a mineshaft
Silence will change to action

May 5, 2015

Orthography.

Early on I learned the difference between Southern Sotho and Northern Sotho. I knew I was working with Southern Sotho.

However, I hadn't taken orthography into consideration. I didn't know orthography was something to take into consideration. Lesotho's versus South Africa's. New York's libraries privileging the latter.

U not O means you. U and O mean you.

This discovery provides much insight. For example, the first word of the piece I am translating and the shortcomings of spelling I am finding/not finding in the dictionary.

I found a source[23] that has three columns for each phrase:

English	Sesotho (South Africa)	Sesotho (Lesotho)
Excuse me	Ntshwarele	Ntsoarele
No	Tjhee	E-e
Yes	Ea	E

The greeting hello is *dumela* in the dictionaries I have been using. Whereas, in the Sesotho of Lesotho it is *lumela*.

"The Sesotho orthography used in Lesotho remains different from the one used in South Africa. In March 1906 a conference was held to discuss the question of a uniform Sesotho orthography for [Lesotho] ... During the colonial period, the issue of adopting the South African orthography was raised ... Each time the question was put forward by the [colonial] government, it was universally rejected by the Basutoland National Council, the paramount chief, and the educated elite" (Rosenberg 214).

May 5th notes, continued

I might have realized this today or on a previous day.

There are no words beginning with the letter c in the dictionary I am using. None beginning with q.

I must confess, I extended my parameters and consulted an online dictionary today, before becoming thoroughly frustrated. Online there are no words beginning with c. However, there are words that begin with q.

To my further dismay, I am now reading the preface to Kriel's *The New Sesotho-English Dictionary*. Yesterday I gleefully engaged in the act of translation with this problematic source.

> "The spelling is in the New Orthography as decided upon by the Joint Language Boards of Transvaal, O.F.S., Bechuanaland and Basutoland, for the purpose of planning a unified orthography. The difficulty of the various dialects is a grave one, but fortunately not insuperable, and the editor is convinced that, with patience and tact, the whole cluster of Sotho-Chwana Languages can be merged into one unified Sesotho Language for the Union of South Africa. That this book should prove to be a step in that direction is the editor's sincere desire."

Basutoland was the name given to Lesotho by the colonial government. This dictionary is declaring its orthographic authority for all speakers of Sesotho in South Africa, Botswana and Lesotho. However, the people of Lesotho never approved it. There is more to the controversy than I am currently able to access.[24]

Preface

This book is the outcome of a wish expressedby Dr. Eiselen, some time Chief Inspector of Native Education in Transvaal, and now Secretary of Native Affairs.

When the compiler submitted the manuscript of his previous dictionary —"Sotho-Afrikaanse Woordeboek"—in 1941 to the Sesotho Language Board in Pretoria, Dr. Eiselen, then chairman of the Board, asked him on behalf of the Board to provide a Northern Sesotho-English Dictionary.

It was not without some hesitation that the compiler undertook this task, realising that there were men more capable than himself who could have done so.

Once started, he proceeded unceasingly, culling from every available source, and spending many hours with the Basotho, especially those of the older generation. In his task he was greatly assisted by students of the Native Training Institution at Bothšabêlô, Middelburg, Tvl.

Books to which the writer has referred, with much gratitude, are such as J. T. Brown's "Secwana-English Dictionary"; "Sesuto-English Dictionary," by A. Mabille and H. Dieterlen; "English-Sesuto Vocabulary," by A. Casalis; "School Dictionary," by Kritzinger and Steyn; Webster's "Collegiate Dictionary"; Chambers's "Twentieth Century Dictionary" and "Die Groot Woordeboek", by Kritzinger, Steyn, Schoonees and Cronjé.

In addition, the editor has great pleasure in acknowledging his personal obligations to Miss Decima E. Snell of London, for kindly reading the English proofs.

SPELLING —The spelling is in the New Orthography, as decided upon by the Joint Language Boards of Transvaal, O.F.S., Bechuanaland and Basutoland, for the purpose of planning a unified orthography.

DIALECTS —The difficulty of the various dialects is a grave one, but fortunately not insuperable, and the editor is convinced that, with patience and tact, the whole cluster of Sotho-Chwana Languages can be merged into one unified Sesotho Language for the Union of South Africa. That this book should prove to be a step in that direction is the editor's sincere desire.

REVISION —This book is now revised; many obsolete words and phrases discarded and new words and terms enlisted.

One of the first reactions of the European explorers and colonists, on being confrontedb y a world that was wholly novel and outside the bounds of their experience, was to reorder it according to their existing structure ofk nowledge. This entailedi mposingt heir intellectualg rid on the unfamiliar masso f detailt hat surroundedt hem. Linguistica nd otherb ordersa nd boundariesw ere erectedi n ordert o restructuret he Africanw orld in a way thatw ould make it more comprehensiblet o Europeans. Once linguistic expertsh ad anchoredl anguagess patially,b y erectingb ordersa round regularitieos f their grammara nd vocabulary,t hey sought to stabilizet hem over time by tracing their historical roots.[25]

The formatting of the above quote was mere chance. It was the result of copying and pasting from an internet source into a Word document. But it made so much sense, still legible, but distorted. Like a (post)colonial reality. Like *Black Sunlight.*

Translation attempt continued

"Bophelo bo naka li maripa" by Lits'oanelo Yvonne Nei

Ea (*yes*) re (*we*) likolo (*school?*) li (*?*) phomoletse (*phomo—graphite used to decorate clay, phomola—be on holiday, phomolo—rest, holiday; letse—to lie, has lain down*) keresemese (*kerese—candle, mese—. . . ; internet find—Christmas*) hoa (*shout, call, cheer, exult, foam, froth, roar, hiss*) fihla (*arrive*) motseng (*motse—village*) mohlankana (*young man*) oa (*you are*) seithati (*egoist, selfish*) a tsoa Belekomo. E mochitja ea litšika-tšika (*sika—take, carry a child; lesika—family; tshika—sinew, lineage, generation*), a tsamaea (*tsamaya—go, walk, march*) ka (*about*) boqhetseke bohle (*all*), pono (*sight, view, vision*) e ntle ruri. Ka hanong teng e le kheleke. Khele, ka lumela ho nkeha maikutlo ke eena etsoe o ile a nkatamela boo! Ra tšepisana maholimo le mafatše hoo ke ileng ka utloa hore sekolo se tla salla ba se ratang, ha e le 'na ke ne ke sala tjaka eo morao. Re ile ra rera ho tsoa ka la pholo-khoaba. Nkhono a qhoeloa habohloko ke taba eo, hoo a neng a kene sepetlele ke pelo bohloko.

Yes we school holiday christmas cheer arrive village young man you selfish a tsoa Belekomo.[26] E mochitja ea carry a child, the family, generation, go walk about boqhetseke all, vision e ntle ruri.

Monday, May 11, 2015

Liepollo,

You would be sad to know about my country right now. Six police officers in the city of Baltimore—not too far from Washington, D.C.—caused the injuries of a young man that led to his death. The reason he was apprehended by police officers was because he started running when he saw them. We can assume he was scared. He had reason to be scared. They severed his spine. The police department is saying the officers did nothing wrong. They are saying the young man caused his own injuries. They are standing by it.

We think apartheid is over only to see it manifest from under a cloak. Like silhouettes, the ghosts of white supremacy are ever-present, unseen puppet masters. Exposure is frequent these days, in my country, but there are too many who refuse to see, to speak, to listen, to feel.

"Racism is being recycled in new and old forms. The fate of Africa is the fate of the diaspora," Mbembe says.

What is my function? I am not mere bystander critiquing orthographic politics and the violent gift of literacy. I am a writer. A speaker of English. I am not a translator or a speaker of Sesotho. What right do I have to embark on this project? An emotional pang—is that a right?

> To decide whether you are prepared enough to start translating, then, it might help if you have graduated into speaking, by choice or preference, of intimate matters in the language of the original.

Gayatri, do you condemn me?

> In my view, the translator from a third world language should be sufficiently in touch with what is going on in literary production in that language and be capable of distinguishing between good and bad writing by women, resistant and conformist writing by women.

I'll take that as a yes. But, Gayatri, are you saying bad women writers shouldn't be translated? I mean, I can't tell if the story I was translating is bad or good, in your opinion. I do not know if it was political and deconstructing women's roles in postcolonial society. Resistant to what and conforming to whom? Of course we could debate the politics of self-expression; and the definition of good and bad, as abstract concepts, or as applied to women writers. I think Devi is a bad writer, or maybe I don't like your translation, but I think she is important. Thank you for translating her resistant prose. And, maybe, my aesthetic has been colonized.

> I choose Devi because she is unlike her scene ... I remain interested in writers who are against the current, against the mainstream. I remain convinced that the interesting literary text might be precisely the text where you do not learn what the majority view of majority cultural

> representation or self-representations of a nation state might be.

That would be hard to do without a depth of knowledge in the culture, the language and literature.

> Without a sense of the rhetoricity of language, a species of neocolonialist construction of the non-Western scene is afoot. No argument for convenience can be persuasive here.

Was it convenience I was after? I didn't use the wrong dictionaries out of convenience.

> Learning about translation on the job, I came to think that it would be a practical help if one's relationship with the language being translated was such that sometimes one preferred to speak in it about intimate things.

I'm unsure if this has been an act of violence or an act of love. Gayatri, I never thought I could succumb to translation, I knew that. Things may have been different if I had been able to access the orthography, if the spellings of the words I was searching for corresponded to the spellings of the words in the dictionary. I thought maybe I could grasp a distorted understanding of the piece.

Is it possible to not engage in violence—when everything I have, everything I am, is its product? How does the artist/friend avoid perpetuating the violence into which we are almost all born? If we make beauty of violence, is it worth it?[27]

Liepollo!

I have a friend in town. You'd love her. We were talking about language yesterday. About swearing in other languages. Her first love was Filipina so she knows how to say *Your sister is a whore* in Tagalog. She pronounced it slowly for me.

"Is there a Spanish influence? It sounds Spanish."

"Yes," she replied.

I wonder if there was a way to say your sister is a whore in Tagalog before colonialism. Or did this perspective arrive with Catholicism?

And why don't the dictionaries at least state their dialect, their orthography, clearly? On the cover. In bold letters.

Because heterogeneity is not valued.
Linguistic homogeny is a pursuit of hegemony.

"The spirit of a culture lies in its language," Ngũgĩ says.

Chronology

Circa 2 million years ago Early hominids in eastern and southern Africa.

Circa 100,000 years ago Stone Age peoples in southern Africa.

Circa 6000 BCE Hunter-gatherers inhabit southern Africa, including portions of Lesotho.

1200–1400 Predecessors of Sotho-speaking people move into Transvaal region of South Africa.

1550 Fokeng cross Vaal River into modern Orange Free State.

1600 Fokeng settle in Mohokare Valley.

1700s Basotho chiefs begin to exercise power within small-scale communities.

1720 Mohlomi is born.

1786 Moshoeshoe, eldest son of Mokhachane's first house, is born at Menkhoaneng.

1804 Moshoeshoe is circumcised and changes his name from Lepoqo to Letlama, "the Binder."

1806 Peete takes his grandson, Moshoeshoe, to meet the famous chief and rainmaker, Mohlomi.

1809 After successfully raiding cattle from RaMonaheng, Letlama becomes known by his self-proclaimed new name, Moshoeshoe.

1810 Moshoeshoe marries 'MaMahato, daughter of Bafokeng chief Seepheephe.

1811 Letsie (Mohato), the eldest son of Moshoeshoe's first house, is born.

1816 Mohlomi dies.

1821 *Lifaqane* reaches Lesotho with invasion by Mpangazitha and Matiwane.

from: Zahra Patterson
to: Liepollo Rantekoa
date: June 9 2010
subject: (no subject)

where is my little friend?

from: Liepollo Rantekoa
to: Zahra Patterson
date: June 17 2010
subject: (no subject)

your little friend is broke, trying to get her life together and all in all feeling like shit. my sister is getting married on the 26th june hence the delay…fuck, ama rant given you 'kinda' asked: why the fuck at my age can i not motivate myself and squander money like a bitch?!
am in lesotho right now.

more importantly, how are you?

love

from: Zahra Patterson
to: Liepollo Rantekoa
date: June 19 2010
subject: (no subject)

One day we'll go walking in Lesotho. We'll be in our 40s and generally "okay" with our lives. And we'll laugh about how screwed up our mid-late 20s fucking were.
Today, I'm doing really well. Everything's daily in my life. The ups and downs.
I hope you're looking forward to your sister's wedding. It will be beautiful, surely.

I'm going to Detroit on Monday, just for a week. It will be nice to take a vacation and there's a big Forum going on there. We can change the world and make it better.

lots of love

Attachments

A note on the attachments

I did my best to preserve the authenticity of Rantekoa's original documents, as sent to me via email. However, the press release and review have been shortened, the layout and background have been changed on the press release, and slight edits were made for purposes of consistency.

I.

THE UNCOMFORTABLE GAZE by Liepollo Rantekoa

It is 18h30 and I was standing in a long winding queue that snaked out of the yard. I am at the local /neighborhood shop. There is a lingering smell of paraffin mixed with the scent of hard labour in the air. Then it hits me. This moment is also known as the 'aha moment' by Oprah fans. Everybody else in the queue or being served is buying household essential goods like a can of beans, piltchards, maybe two tomatoes and onion; phofo ya papa, one tea bag and/or paraffin. The carriers of their goods are their wrought hands indicating their occupation and as such their level of economical class. And me? I am there to purchase a nonsensical 'need': a cigarette. It is clear that I was an exception from my fellow queue comrades: my dressing, my non-participation in general talk; my insistence on personal space and body language. The other clients, however, are patiently waiting for their turn to be served; passing time with local news under the evening sky. On another day I am at the mall, purchasing the same product. However, here I feel safe in the environment; the latter also works hard to serve my comfort. Here, there are options of products and multiple paying points. The air here is pleasant and not stifled by the sweat of hard earned money but by perfumed hard earned money. Purchasing here is done by using a basket or trolley as a carrier; goods are bought in large quantities; and pleasantries are passed to acknowledge membership of a class of a few. This is the Lesotho we live in today. The first group had to wait for the end of the day, when family members come together and contribute to the needs of the house - these needs are determined by the monies collected that day. The 'mall' group, however, need not wait for the end of the day, nor any day for that matter, before household purchases are made.

As I left the mall store, I recognize a face from the neighbourhood shop. The person sees me too; however the social environment does not allow us to make any further contact. Buying power has drawn the line clearly, that does not allow for any kind of interaction between the two of us. After meditating on the incident, I recall how Basotho are known to be humble people; class not interfering nor determining interaction. If the current incidents are anything to go by, it seems as if our humility has us in a cockhold. This kind of humility infiltrates, whether voluntarily or not, so deep into the person that it peppers conversation and negates personal itineraries. This depressed humility is felt by all and contributed to by all. It eats away daily at the essence of a person, to a point that you forget yourself and the teachings of old. A couple of steps ahead I turn back and greet the person because as the old adage notes: tumeliso ha e fele.

---

tumeliso ha e fele "means" one cannot buy a greeting

II.

PRESS RELEASE: *BA RE E NERE*...LITFEST (MARCH 2011)

The choice is ours
So is the mind and the matches too
The choice is ours
So is the beginning...
The choice is ours
So is the need and the want too
The choice is ours
So is the vision of the day

Extract from Keorapetse Kgositsile's poem "If I Could Sing" (Kwela Publishers, 2002)

Literature is an ongoing conversation that engages a politics of friendship; a process of discussion and discovery that takes place across multiple platforms and in various spaces and contexts. Literature also cannot be confined to a provincial way of relating to, expressing, narrating and even acknowledging it. The role of extra-textual references also cannot be ignored when engaging in literary discourse. The *Ba re e nere*...Litfest (March 2011) seeks to encourage discourse on these factors.

In Lesotho, writers and musos such as Thomas Mofolo, Polo 'Malehlohonolo, Patrick Bereng, Morabo Morojele, Mpho Brown, Bhudaza, and Mary Bosiu to name but a few have provided nourishing text reflective of, amongst others, their cultural roots and social influences whilst other renowned writers such as Njabulo Ndebele, Keorapetse Kgositsile, Zakes Mda and Ayi Kwei Armah have suckled from Lesotho's bosom to become who they are and what they write about today. The *Ba re e nere*...Litfest (March 2011) pays homage to literatis by exploring their work and experiences through the access to *Chimurenga Library* at the Vodacom Internet Shop (Maseru, Lesotho), screening of audio-visual material as well as the hosting of weekly discussions throughout the month of March 2011 in Lesotho.

King Moshoeshoe I noted, *ntoa boholo kea hosane* and as such the *Ba re e nere*...Litfest seeks to acknowledge Basotho and other pan African authors, learn and share knowledge within and across geopolitical borders as well as encourage a literary discourse in Lesotho for the tales of tomorrow reflect the etchings of those from the past that are daily impressioned on, recounted and re-written by the authors, distributors, vendors, artists, printers, institutions and readers alike.

The *Ba re e nere*...Litfest (March 2011) is conceptualised and curated by Liepollo Rantekoa

For more info:
[Tel.] +266 59738858
[Email] lesothobooks@gmail.com
[Facebook] Ba Re Literature

Sponsors
Alliance Francaise, Maseru (Lesotho); Morija Museum and Archives (Lesotho); Nhlahlapa Architects; Meditteranneé: Pizzeria Restaurant & The Coffee Shop, Maseru (Lesotho); Pioneer Office National, Maseru (Lesotho); Tee Tee Chemicals & Equipment (pty) ltd.; Vodacom Internet Shop, Maseru (Lesotho); Ster Kinekor; Maseru (Lesotho); Nemisis Inc.

Audio-visual screenings
Material provided by *Chimurenga* Magazine, Jimmy Rage, Kgafela oa Magogodi, Lesego Rampolokeng and Peace Corp

III.

PART 1

Denigrate

Pull -

Down

Oppress

Melanin

Excuses

Labels

Dehumanise

Other

PART 2

Title: Bantu Ghost

Author: Lesego RAMPOLOKENG

Unabashed in critiquing his living experiences, whether institutional or personal, are some ways to describe Lesego RAMPOLOKENG's productions. A poet, filmmaker and producer, RAMPOLOKENG ventures to "speak backwards" using movement in brief liners, prompting the reader to explore some valuable references in *Bantu Ghost: a stream of (black) unconsciousness*.

Poetic chapters included in the scripted book, *Bantu Ghost*, are The Cell, The Tower of Bable, Chaining the Mind, The Black Word, The New World Hoarder, and The Search for Consciousness. The text's style may seem haphazard and a whirlwind to read for some. However, his poetic styles encompass the scholastic cinquain, epigpram and free verse also exemplifying punctuality in its delivery. Whether the text is read out loud or silently, the words are jarring, descriptively layered yet simply lean.

This strategy was probably intentional as the script deals with what would commonly be considered sensitive socio-cultural, political and id matters.

Furthermore, the script was written, produced and performed by RAMPOLOKENG for stage—a feat complimented by the contribution of Nelisiwe XABA's experimental choreography and Bobby RODWELL on co-production.

Bantu Ghost is a read suited to your poetry bibliophiles, experimental musos, theatrical literati and politico-philosophy fundis as well as the unconscious adventurers.

Appendix 1

The Black Panther Party tends to be known for a handful of radical leaders and their revolutionary ideology. But it was the collective action of many members that made the Party so valuable to black communities, and so threatening to the United States.

> One of the other core demands of the Program was direct democratic community control of not only the police but the legal system. Fifty years ago, the Panthers were already proclaiming, "We want an immediate end to POLICE BRUTALITY and MURDER of black people." One must wonder what would have happened if millions had followed the strategies they proposed rather than the path of slogans, street protests and the lobbying of politicians that has prevailed. The immediate Panther response to police oppression and brutality was a combination of self-education and direct action. They thought it essential for all members of the community to "know their rights," but their position was that the whole community also had to act directly to enforce those rights. Foner notes that "the Party established a system of armed patrol cars, completely legal, carrying both guns and lawbooks," so that "whenever black men or women were stopped by the police, armed Panthers would be on the scene, making sure that their constitutional rights were not violated."[i]
>
> A more long-term goal involved developing a political movement and detailed plan for community control of police. The plan is outlined in a "Petition Statement for Community Control of Police."[ii] It would involve "establishing police departments for the major communities of any city." This was to include all local communities, though the particular focus was obviously on enabling major oppressed ethnic (or class) communities to control their own affairs. Control of the police would be in the hands

of neighborhood councils elected by the citizens of the neighborhoods. The councils would determine policies for the community police departments. The administration of these departments would be carried out by police commissions whose members would be "selected by a Neighborhood Police Control Council," which would have fifteen members elected by the community. Councils would have disciplinary power over the police and set policies for the commissions and departments to carry out. The council would have the power to recall the commissioners and the community would have the power to recall the council members. All police officers would come from the communities they serve. The result of all these proposals would be effective power of the community over the police and policing.

This excerpt is from "Power to the Community: The Black Panthers' Living Legacy of Grassroots Organization" by John P. Clark, published on his blog *It Is What It Isn't*.

i. Philip S. Foner, *The Black Panthers Speak* (Philadelphia and New York: J.B. Lippincott Co., 1970), pp. xvii-xviii.

ii. "Petition Statement for Community Control of Police. Summary of Police Control Amendment that Must Be Established in the Cities and Communities of America to End Fascism," in *The Black Panther* (June 14, 1969); reprinted in *The Black Panthers Speak*, p. 179.

Notes

1 The event was a Women of Color reading in Pratt Institute's Alumni Hall. Curated by Mahogany L. Browne and video recorded by Stephon Lawrence.

2 Two days later, January 9, 2011, this piece was published on Kagablog of Kaganof.com, a project of African Noise Foundation.

3 *Sesotho Online* "General Introduction." See also *South African History Online* (www.sahistory.org) for a comprehensive overview of the different peoples and languages of South Africa and bordering countries—while colonial powers drew borders, people and traditions have always blurred them.

4 From Clement Doke's article "Bantu Language Pioneers of the Nineteenth Century." *Bantu Studies*, 14, 3. 1940, revised 1961, p. 36.

5 Moeshoeshoe I (c. 1786–1870) is considered the founder of the Basotho people, and welcomed the French missionaries along with new crops and technologies. "Because the emerging culture was largely pragmatic and flexible, not ideological and dogmatic, the Basotho swiftly embraced many innovations … However, the challenge of Boer farmers staking claims to Basotho land and of Cape officials seeking to annex it was far more difficult" (Rosenberg 5). While the King enjoyed seeing his language in print, he objected to the reduction of many local dialects into a single orthography; words that should be attributed to other people were attributed to his people (Coplan 8).

6 From Doke's "Scripture Translation into Bantu Languages." *African Studies*, 17, 2. 1958, revised 1961, p. 114. What the missionary-linguists, Casalis, Arbousset, and others deemed as the gift of a Protestant connection to God was in fact a gift to world literature: "[I]t was difficult to prevent gifted newly-literates from experimenting with writing of their own" (Gérard 63). An act of violence: the gift of writing.

7 Copied from *A Multilingual Illustrated Dictionary* by John Bennet and Nthuseng Tsoeu. Pharos, 2006, p. 303.

8 The words in this glossary are from the website barelitfest.com. Ba re e ne re, originally a literary festival created and coordinated by Liepollo Rantekoa, continued after her untimely death. Zachary Rosen and Lineo Segoete added a website and a number of other literary moments to the foundations Rantekoa had laid. For example, they publish short stories by writers from Lesotho. They also created a dictionary, with which they are adding words to the Sesotho dictionary.

9 Nei's story was originally published on March 5, 2015 by Ba re e ne re. The complete original version can be read there. See Works Cited for the full link.

10 From *Singing Away the Hunger: The Autobiography of an African Woman* by Mpho 'M'atsepo Nthunya. University of Natal Press, 1996, p. 1.

11 Ibid, p. 69.

12 See Appendix I for further reading on the community organizing principles of The Black Panthers.

13 From *Orality and Literacy: The Technologizing of the Word* by Walter J. Ong. Psychology Press, 1982, p. 7.

14 "Queer Futures" was hosted at The Green Space at WNYC on May 8, 2015.

15 *Chimurenga*: a pan-African platform of writing, art and politics founded by Ntone Edjabe in 2002. Drawing together a myriad voices from across Africa and the diaspora, *Chimurenga* takes many forms, operating as an innovative platform for free ideas and political reflection about Africa by Africans.

16 Binyavanga Wainaina's words are taken from "Opening Night: The Future is Now" on May 4th, 2015 at The Great Hall at Cooper Union.

17 I found this article on the Facebook page of one of Liepollo's friends, whom I've never met. She is a vocal activist for the rights of Black students in South Africa.

18 "Smuts, Jan Christiaan (1870–1950). A soldier, intellectual, and statesmen … was prime minister of South Africa from 1919 to 1924 and from 1939 to 1948 … For all his intellectual brilliance, Smuts failed to recognize the injustice of racial segregation" (Saunders 232).

19

20 Images from Hamel's one-way, six-volume dictionary.

21 From Kriel's dictionary.

22 Using Kriel's *The New Sesotho-English Dictionary,* Afrikaanse Press, 1950.

23 From "Basic Phrases" in Sesotho Online by J.A.K. Olivier. http://www.sesotho.web.za/phrases.htm. Accessed August 2017.

24 Trying to get ahold of an article called "The Sotho Orthographies: Yesterday, Today and Tomorrow" by T.B. Bing. But I'm not having luck. Sent request. Hoping CUNY has access to Taylor and Francis which is holding the article hostage. But then, I don't even know if it will ultimately be what I hope it to be. Six months later, a chance occurrence led me to the article. The article doesn't discuss the reasons for the different orthographies in South Africa and Lesotho; it discusses the different orthographies between Tswana, Pedi, and Sesotho. However, I did discover that it was in 1959, under the Bantu Education Act (1947), that South Africa established its own orthography. "[T]his political and emotional issue has led to and continues to produce problems both for teachers and students of Sesotho, as well as for authors writing in Sesotho and their reading public" (Demuth 3).

25 From "The Roots of Ethnicity: Discourse and the Politics of Language Construction in South-East Africa." by Patrick Harries, *African Affairs,* vol. 87, issue 346, p. 26.

26 Belekomo here may be referring to Belekomo Pass, which is a pedestrian route on Mount Machache.

27 Spivak quotes from "The Politics of Translation." *Outside in the Teaching Machine* (Routledge 1993) pp. 187, 188, 189, 181, 183 respectively.

Works Cited

"About Us." *Chimurenga*. www.chimurenga.co.za.

Ashby, Muata. *Egyptian Yoga: The Philosophy of Englightenment*. Sema Institute, 1997.

Ba re e ne re Literature Festival. www.barelitfest.com.

Bennett, John and Nthuseng Tsoeu. *Multilingual Illustrated Dictionary: Dictionary Isichazimazwi Bukantswe Isichazi-magama Bukafoko Woordeboek Pukuntšu*. Pharos, 2006.

Burrows, Vinie, Boubacar Boris Diop, Yusef Komunyakaa, Achille Mbembe, Ngũgĩ wa Thiong'o and Rashidah Ismaili. "The Witnesses: What is the Value of Age and Wisdom?" 7 May 2015, Bronx Museum of Art, Bronx, NY. *PEN World Voices Festival*.

Buuck, David. "African Doppelganger: Hybridity and Identity in the Work of Dambudzo Marechera." *Research in African Literatures*, vol. 28, no. 2, 1997, pp. 118–131. JSTOR, www.jstor.org/stable/3820447.

Bwesigye. "Twitter Status." 25 December 2015. https://twitter.com/bwesigye/status/680526741195112448.

"Cheers and Protest as University of Cape Town Removes Cecil Rhodes Statue." Agence France-Presse in Cape Town. 9 April 2015. *The Guardian*. https://www.theguardian.com/world/2015/apr/09/university-cape-town-removes-statue-cecil-rhodes-celebration-afrikaner-protest.

Clark, John P. "Power to the Community: The Black Panthers' Living Legacy of Grassroots Organization." *It Is What It Isn't*, Changing Suns Press, 25 Nov. 2015, www.changingsunspress.com/it-is-what-it-isnt.

Coplan, David B. "The Meaning of Sesotho." *Journal of Research: Sesotho Language and Culture*. National University of Lesotho, 1992.

Daymond, M. J. "Self-Translation, Untranslatability, and Postcolonial Community in the Autobiographies of Mpho Nthunya and Agnes Lottering." *English in Africa*, vol. 33, no. 2, 2006, pp. 91–111. JSTOR, www.jstor.org/stable/40232382.

Demuth, Katherine. "Unifying Organizational Principles in the Development of Orthographic Conventions." African Studies Center, Boston, MA. 1989. http://www.cog.brown.edu/people/demuth/articles/1989DemuthMoz.pdf.

Doke, Clement M. "Bantu Language Pioneers of the Nineteenth Century." 1940. *The Southern Bantu Languages.* The International African Institute by Dawsons of Pall Mall, 1967.

---. "Scripture Translation into Bantu Languages." 1958. *The Southern Bantu Languages*. The International African Institute by Dawsons of Pall Mall, 1967.

Gérard, Albert S. *Contexts of African Literature*. Editions Rodopi, 1990.

Hamel, L. *English-Southern Sesotho Dictionary*, vol. 1-6. Catholic Center: 1965.

Harries, Patrick. "The Roots of Ethnicity: Discourse and the Politics of Language Construction in South-East Africa." *African Affairs*, vol. 87, no. 346, 1988, pp. 25–52. JSTOR, www.jstor.org/stable/722808.

Kriel, T. J. *The New Sesotho-English Dictionary*. Afrikaanse Press, 1950.

Marechera, Dambudzo. *Black Sunlight*. 1980. Penguin African Writers, 2009.

Mda, Zakes. *The Whale Caller*. Penguin, 2005.

Nei, Yvonne Lits'oanelo. "Bophelo bo naka li maripa." Ba re e ne re, 2015. bareenere.com/2015/03/05/short-story-bophelo-bo-naka-li-maripa-by-litsoanelo-yvonne-nei.

Nthunya, Mpho ′M′atsepo. *Singing Away the Hunger: The Autobiography of an African Woman*. University of Natal Press, 1996.

Olivier, J.A.K. "Basic Phrases." *Sesotho Online*, 2009, www.sesotho.web.za/phrases.htm. Accessed 5 May 2015.

Ong, Walter. *Orality and Literacy: The Technologizing of the Word*. Psychology Press, 1982.

Rampolokeng, Lesego. *Bantu Ghost: A Stream of (Black) Unconsciousness*. Adlib Studio, 2009.

Rosenberg, Scott and Richard F. Weisfelder. *Historical Dictionary of Lesotho: Second Edition.* The Scarecrow Press, 2013.

Saunders, Christopher and Nicholas Southey. *Historical Dictionary of South Africa: Second Edition*. Scarecrow Press, 2000.

Spivak, Gayatri Chakravorty. "The Politics of Translation." *Outside in the Teaching Machine*. Routledge, 1993.

Thiong'o, Ngũgĩ wa. *Decolonising the Mind*. 1981. Heinemann, 2005.

Wainaina, Binyavanga. "Opening Night: The Future is Now." 4 May 2015. The Great Hall at Cooper Union, New York, NY. *PEN World Voices Festival.*

---, Zanele Muholi, Kehinde Bademosi and Shireen Hassim. "Queer Futures." 8 May 2015. The Green Space at WNYC, New York, NY. *PEN World Voices Festival.* https://livestream.com/thegreenespace/events/4025386.

Acknowledgments

Thank you, Chuck Kuan, Anna Moschovakis, Rebekah Smith, and everyone at Ugly Duckling Presse.

Chronology was inspired by Theresa Hak Kyung Cha's *Dictee*, M. NourbeSe Philip's *Zong!*, Sawako Nakayasu's *Mouth: Eats Color*, and Wangechi Mutu's artwork.

I am deeply indebted to Ngũgĩ wa Thiong'o for his postcolonial theory and writings, and to my mother, Catherine Patterson (née Murphy), who raised me with an anti-colonial perspective and an interest in language justice.

Thank you for successive readings and continued support, Sarah Riggs, Mendi Obadike, and E. Tracy Grinnell.

Thank you, Laura Elrick and my family.

Gayatri Chakravorty Spivak, thank you for the imagined conversation. And all the additional voices that comprise this book: Lits'oanelo Yvonne Nei, Mendi+Keith Obadike, Vinie Burrows, Boubacar Boris Diop, Yusef Komunyaaka, Achille Mbembe, Ngũgĩ wa Thiong'o, Rashidah Ismaili, Binyavanga Wainaina, Zanele Muholi, Kehinde Bademosi, Shireen Hassim, Walter Ong, Zakes Mda, Mpho 'M'atsepo Nthunya, Patrick Harries, and John P. Clark.

Liepollo Rantekoa and Dambudzo Marechera.

Chronology was supported by a Watershed Lab residency at Mount Tremper Arts, with lead support by the National Endowment for the Arts.